X-TREME FACTS: ANCIENT HISTORY

ANCIENT CHINA

by Catherine C. Finan

BEARPORT PUBLISHING

Minneapolis, Minnesota

Credits:
© Title page, 17 bottom, GuoZhongHua/Shutterstock; 4 top, Harvepino/Shutterstock; 4 bottom, Katoosha/Shutterstock; 4 bottom middle, matrioshka/Shutterstock; 5 top, Hung Chung Chih/Shutterstock; 5 top right, windmoon/Shutterstock; 5 middle, luchschenF/Shutterstock; 5 bottom, Dragon Images/Shutterstock; 6 top, Shan_shan/Shutterstock.com; 6 bottom, Vyaznov/Shutterstock; 6 bottom left, Dmitry Chulov/Shutterstock.com; 6 bottom middle, salajean/Shutterstock.com; 6 bottom right, Aisyaqilumaranas/Shutterstock.com; 6 bottom lower right, /Shutterstock; Somchai Boonpun; 7 top, 7 bottom, 8 bottom, 11 top, 20 bottom, A Special Exhibition of Paintings on "Up the River During Qingming" in the Museum Collection (exhibit). Taipei: National Palace Museum/Public Domain; 7 top left, 20 bottom left, 20 bottom right, 21 top middle, 26 bottom right, Album of the Yongzheng Emperor in Costumes/Public Domain; 7 top right, ShutterOK/Shutterstock; 7 middle, Public Domain; 7 bottom right, 8 left, 14 bottom right, 27 bottom left, Acquired by Henry Walters, 1915/Public Domain; 7 bottom right, Anonymous Ming Chinese artist/Public Domain; 8 top, BabelStone/Creative Commons; 8 right, Anonymous Ming Chinese artist/Public Domain; 9 top, Meiqianbao/Shutterstock.com; 9 top left, 10 left, 15 bottom, 25 bottom left, William Alexander/Public Domain; 9 top right, 10 right, 12 bottom right, Wellcome Collection gallery/Creative Commons; 9 middle, Gift of Dr. and Mrs. Roger Y. K. Hsu, Dr. Daphne T. Hsu, and Dr. Jeffrey T. Hsu in memory of Robert P. Bergman/Creative Commons; 9 bottom left, Roman Samborskyi/Shutterstock; 9 bottom right, Brocreative/Shutterstock; 10 top, New Africa/Shutterstock; 10 bottom, gyn9037/Shutterstock; 10 top right, Elena Nichizhenova/Shutterstock; 11 lower top, Public Domain; 11 middle left, Melinda Fawver/Shutterstock; 11 bottom, sevenke/Shutterstock; 11 bottom left, Burhan Bunardi/Shutterstock; 12 top, Anonymous artist of the Qing dynasty/Public Domain; 12 bottom , Xiangli Li/Shutterstock.com; 12 left, supermodel/Shutterstock.com; 12 middle, Maggieyang0630/Public Domain; 13 top, elwynn/Shutterstock; 13 lower top, Gary Todd/Creative Commons; 13 top middle, paffy/Shutterstock; 13 bottom, parkisland/Shutterstock.com; 14 top, zhu difeng/Shutterstock; 14–15 bottom, Marti Bug Catcher/Shutterstock; 14 bottom left, Listerning to the Qin, scan by Zhao Ji/Public Domain; 15 top, Dudarev Mikhail/Shutterstock; 15 lower top, feiyuezhangjie/Shutterstock; 15 top left, Olena Yakobchuk/Shutterstock; 15 top right, Public Domain; 16 top, Windmemories/Creative Commons; 16 left, Public Domain; 17 top, Giancarlo Liguori/Shutterstock; 17 top left, Bachkova Natalia/Shutterstock; 17 top right, gan chaonan/Shutterstock; 17 bottom left, Utekhina Anna/Shutterstock; 17 bottom right, Andrey_Kuzmin/Shutterstock; 18 top, r chensiyuan/Creative Commons; 18 bottom, Dennis Jarvis/Creative Commons; 19 bottom, Maros M r a z/Creative Commons; 19 top, Grigvovan/Shutterstock.com; 19 top left, Dmitry Kalinovsky/Shutterstock; 19 top middle, Carlos Adampol Galindo/Creative Commons; 19 top right, Grigvovan/Shutterstock.com; 19 bottom left, cristovao/Shutterstock; 19 bottom middle, Portrait Image Asia/Shutterstock; 19 bottom right, Lopolo/Shutterstock; 20 bottom middle, Tang Yin/Public Domain; 21 top, Nowaczyk/Shutterstock.com; 21 middle, Shan_shan/Shutterstock.com; 21 bottom, Rangan Datta Wiki/Creative Commons; 21 bottom left, iofoto/Shutterstock; 21 bottom right, 1981 Rustic Studio kan/Shutterstock; 22 top, sr.Polyakoff/Shutterstock; 22 bottom, Efired/Shutterstock.com; 22 bottom left, Palace Museum, Beijing/Public Domain; 22 bottom middle, Pratyeka/Creative Commons; 22 bottom right, Peabody Essex Museum/Creative Commons; 23 top, Pavel_D/Shutterstock.com; 23 top left, sirtravelalot/Shutterstock; 23 top right, youyuenyong budsawongkod/Shutterstock.com; 23 bottom, Ewelina W/Shutterstock; 23 bottom left, alexandre zveiger/Shutterstock;23 bottom middle, Mikhail Semenov/Shutterstock.com; 23 bottom right, Gelpi/Shutterstock; 24 top, Sofiaworld/Shutterstock; 24 bottom, Quang nguyen vinh/Shutterstock.com; 24 bottom left, testing/Shutterstock.com; 24 bottom middle, Mahod84/Shutterstock.com; 25 top, Best-Backgrounds/Shutterstock; 25 top left, Kelvin Case/Creative Commons; 25 top right, Protasov AN/Shutterstock; 25 top right middle, timekeep/Shutterstock; 25 bottom, James Michael Dorsey/Shutterstock; 25 bottom middle, NeydtStock/Shutterstock.com; 25 bottom right, Mauro Rodrigues/Shutterstock.com; 26 bottom, HTU/Shutterstock; 27 top, Jasonjung/Dreamstime.com; 27 bottom, paul prescott/Shutterstock.com; 27 bottom right, Amelia Fox/Shutterstock; 28 top left, yxm2008/Shutterstock; 28 left middle, 28 bottom left, xcarrot_007/Shutterstock; 28 middle right, sedir/Shutterstock; 28 bottom right, Kozak Sergii/Shutterstock; 28–29, Austen Photography

President: Jen Jenson
Director of Product Development: Spencer Brinker
Senior Editor: Allison Juda
Associate Editor: Charly Haley
Designer: Colin O'Dea

Developed and produced for Bearport Publishing by BlueAppleWorks Inc.
Managing Editor for BlueAppleWorks: Melissa McClellan
Art Director: T.J. Choleva
Photo Research: Jane Reid

Library of Congress Cataloging-in-Publication Data

Names: Finan, Catherine C., 1972- author.
Title: Ancient China / Catherine C. Finan.
Description: Minneapolis, Minnesota : Bearport Publishing Company, [2022] | Series: X-treme facts: ancient history | Includes bibliographical references and index.
Identifiers: LCCN 2021001098 (print) | LCCN 2021001099 (ebook) | ISBN 9781636910963 (library binding) | ISBN 9781636911038 (paperback) | ISBN 9781636911106 (ebook)
Subjects: LCSH: China--Civilization--Miscellanea--Juvenile literature.
Classification: LCC DS721 .F47 2022 (print) | LCC DS721 (ebook) | DDC 931--dc23
LC record available at https://lccn.loc.gov/2021001098
LC ebook record available at https://lccn.loc.gov/2021001099

Copyright © 2022 Bearport Publishing Company. All rights reserved. No part of this publication may be reproduced in whole or in part, stored in any retrieval system, or transmitted in any form or by any means, electronic, mechanical, photocopying, recording, or otherwise, without written permission from the publisher.

For more information, write to Bearport Publishing, 5357 Penn Avenue South, Minneapolis, MN 55419.
Printed in the United States of America.

Contents

Back in Time to Ancient China

By order of the **emperor**, an army of guards stands watch at a great big wall! The guards scan the northern horizon for any sign of enemies. From east to west, the wall stretches as far as the eye can see. We're in ancient China—one of history's oldest civilizations!

China started about 4,000 years ago along the Yellow River, and it has grown into an incredible culture whose influence is still powerful today. Let's step back in time to explore!

Ancient China's first emperor, Qin Shi Huang, began building the Great Wall about 2,200 years ago.

People in ancient China first ate with chopsticks 4,000 years ago.

People in ancient China were the first to drink tea. They used it as medicine.

Dynamic Dynasties

Imagine having an entire historical period named after you. In ancient China, that's how it worked! Time was marked by the family, or **dynasty**, in power. When an emperor died, his oldest son usually took over. So, how did dynasties change? By force! A new family fought to take control, and a new dynasty began. Each dynasty was marked by its own exciting developments that changed history.

People believed that the emperors were chosen by the gods. But if an emperor ruled badly, the gods would drive him from power, too!

Warriors in the Shang Dynasty were the first to use **bronze** weapons. **These were much stronger than their enemies' stone weapons.**

The umbrella was invented during the Qin Dynasty.

The last emperor of China, Puyi of the Qing Dynasty, **rose to power when he was only three years old.**

Chinese people were the first in the world to invent paper around the second century BCE!

The first toilet paper was made during the Tang Dynasty from tree bark and rags. Not exactly pillowy soft!

Written on Bones

Ancient China's first writings were created during the Shang Dynasty. And what they were written on is just as interesting as what they said. Priests wrote questions about the future on animal bones. Then, they burned the bones and looked at cracks left behind to see if they could find their answers. And that wasn't the only writing. Calligraphy was also invented during the Shang Dynasty. This is a type of writing that uses a brush and ink to make characters that stand for words. Today, China's written language still uses characters.

The bones priests wrote on were called **oracle bones**. Most often, they were ox bones, but sometimes priests used tortoise shells, too.

Emperors used oracle bones to make decisions. They even used them to get weather forecasts!

Ancient Chinese calligraphy was made up of more than 40,000 characters.

Calligraphy artists trained for many years to learn how to write each character perfectly.

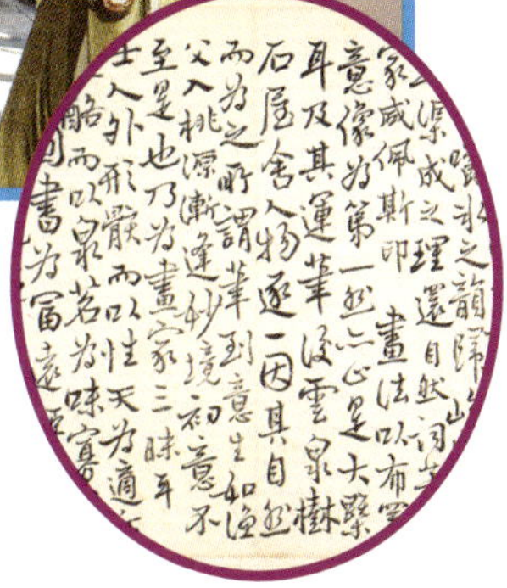

Printing was invented in China more than 1,000 years before it arrived in Europe.

Before inventing paper, ancient Chinese people wrote on thin strips of bamboo and wood. These were sometimes sewn together into a folding book!

A Day in the Life

A priest reading oracle bones or a calligrapher copying down characters would've had an easier life than many other people in ancient China. There was a big gap between the wealthy upper class and the poorer lower class. The wealthy included government workers, **scholars**, and artists, while the lower class was made up of **merchants**, soldiers, and other workers. But, regardless of a person's job, some parts of daily life were the same for just about everybody.

Tea was an important part of daily life across China. It was even used as money!

Silk was very valuable in ancient China. Because merchants were considered the the lowest class of workers, they weren't allowed to wear it.

People in ancient China believed that a person's hair came from their **ancestors**, so it was disrespectful to ever cut it!

A person's body was also considered a gift from their ancestors and had to be respected. That meant no body odor or tattoos!

Ancient Chinese children often **kept crickets as pets.**

Children, parents, and grandparents **all lived in the same house.**

The Emperor Rules!

No matter which job a person had or which class they belonged to, in ancient China the emperor was above everyone—*way* above! Even the emperor's close family members had to be polite and respectful to him at all times. People could not address an emperor as anything other than Your Radiant Highness or Son of Heaven. That meant even his own mother couldn't call him another name!

Qin Shi Huang took over smaller kingdoms and became the first emperor of a **unified** China.

When approaching the emperor's throne, people had to bow down so low that their heads would touch the floor.

The emperor often had many wives, but only one was the empress.

A Great Wall

China's first emperor, Qin Shi Huang, began a wall-building project that would last for centuries. Before him, smaller walls were built across China's northern border to defend against enemies. Qin Shi Huang ordered these to be joined into one massive wall. Soldiers on its many towers kept watch to protect the empire. The dynasties that followed added to it. Today, many parts of the Great Wall still stand!

The Great Wall is the world's longest human-made structure. It is 13,171 miles (21,197 km) long!

About one million people worked on the wall during a period of more than 1,000 years.

Some believe the Great Wall is haunted! Tourists have reported seeing ghosts wandering the wall and even hearing the sound of marching feet.

It's Forbidden!

The Great Wall isn't the only huge building project from China's ancient past. The **Forbidden** City in Beijing is the world's largest ancient palace—and you can still visit it today! Emperor Chengzu, the third emperor of the Ming Dynasty, had the palace **complex** built in the early 1400s. Surrounded by a high wall and wide **moat**, it was designed to protect the emperor from enemies.

It took more than one million workers about 15 years to build the Forbidden City. It has 980 buildings, which include more than 9,000 rooms!

All buildings in the city face south, which symbolized holiness. The north stood for enemies and evil!

People could only enter the Forbidden City with the emperor's permission. Anyone who entered without it could be killed!

The Forbidden City's roofs were built so birds can't land on them. No messy bird poop here!

When it was built, the Forbidden City had no toilets! Instead, people peed and pooped in pots that were then emptied outside of the city.

Today, the Forbidden City is **home to more than 100 cats!**

An Army for the Afterlife

Emperor Chengzu's Forbidden City is the world's largest palace, but Emperor Qin Shi Huang wins the prize for the world's biggest tomb. The emperor started having his tomb built when he took power at age 13. It grew to about the size of a football field. And what's inside might be even more impressive. An army of more than 8,000 **terra-cotta** soldiers—along with life-size chariots and horses—joined the emperor in his tomb to protect him in the afterlife!

The emperor's tomb is part of a cemetery that covers 22 square miles (57 sq km)— about half the size of Disney World!

It took about 700,000 workers almost 40 years to build the tomb!

Qin Shi Huang had many workers killed during the tomb's construction so they wouldn't tell people where it was being built!

The emperor's huge and crowded **tomb was discovered by farmers digging a well.**

No two statues in the terra-cotta army are alike. Each has a unique set of features and armor.

The tomb contained **crossbows** that **were set to shoot arrows at anyone who entered.**

Life Goes On

Qin Shi Huang's tomb and life-size army may be unusual, but they reflected ancient Chinese beliefs about death. People believed that after a person died, they continued to live in the afterlife. So, tombs contained things people would need in this new life, such as weapons, clothing, and food.

The people of ancient China also believed in a spirit world where ancestors lived with the gods. It was important to stay on your dead relatives' good side . . . or things could get rough!

Some tombs contained mirrors, which were believed to protect people from evil.

People wanted snacks and refreshments for the afterlife, too! Animal-shaped **vessels** for food and drinks were buried with the dead.

Every spring, people in modern China still clean up their ancestors' graves and make offerings during the Tomb Sweeping Festival.

Land of the Dragon

Along with the afterlife and the spirit world, the people of ancient China held strong beliefs about the power of symbols, numbers, and colors. The most powerful symbol was the dragon, which was thought to rule over water and weather. It was the emperor's personal symbol. The **phoenix**, which represented goodness and grace, symbolized the empress. The number nine was also associated with the emperor, as was the color yellow. And that's just the start of it. . . .

Many emperors believed they were **descendants** of dragons!

The color red represented good luck and was worn by brides in ancient China. White was associated with **mourning** and was worn at funerals.

The Chinese word for eight sounds like the word for prosper, so eight was considered the luckiest number in ancient China.

The number four was considered the unluckiest number. The word for it sounds like the word for death!

Even today, some people in China will pay more for a home with an address that has a lucky number!

Top-Secret Silk

Because the dragon was a symbol for the emperor, it was a pretty big deal. It made its way into many kinds of ancient Chinese art. One of the most important art forms was silk making, which used silkworm cocoons to make silk thread. The thread was then dyed and woven into beautiful patterns to make silk cloth that was traded throughout Asia and Europe. But because it was no ordinary cloth, the process of making it was kept secret for more than 1,000 years!

An unbroken **strand of silk can be more than half a mile (0.8 km) long!**

To make silk, cocoons were steamed, rinsed, and unwound. The fibers were then combined into threads and woven into cloth.

Silk was so valuable, some dynasties used it as money!

Trade routes connecting China with the Middle East and Europe were called the Silk Road, named for the most popular good traded along it.

Two Europeans smuggled silkworm eggs out of China in 550. The secret was out . . . and so were the silkworms!

In ancient China, **anyone who shared the secret of how to make silk was put to death!**

Ancient China Lives On

From the yellow silk robes of its emperors to its enormous Great Wall, ancient China's civilization might seem like the distant past—but its last emperor ruled into the twentieth century. This makes China the longest continuous civilization in the history of the world! And we should thank the people of ancient China for many of the inventions and innovations that make our lives better today.

People in ancient China were **the first to use paper money!**

Gunpowder was invented in China to be used in bombs, guns, rockets . . . and fireworks!

Chinese people made the first firecrackers. The loud noise was thought to scare away evil spirits.

People in ancient China invented the first earthquake detector!

Ice cream was invented 2,200 years ago in China. This sweet treat was a mix of milk, snow, and rice.

Chinese Slat Book

Craft Project

Before the invention of paper, the people of ancient China wrote on long, narrow strips of wood or bamboo. Each strip was about as long as one chopstick and as wide as two. For longer writings, many strips could be sewn together to make a fold-up book. Go old-school and create your own ancient Chinese fold-up book!

Making books from strips of bamboo took many hours.

What You Will Need

- 5 craft sticks
- A black marker
- String
- Scissors

Step One

Use a black marker to write on five craft sticks.

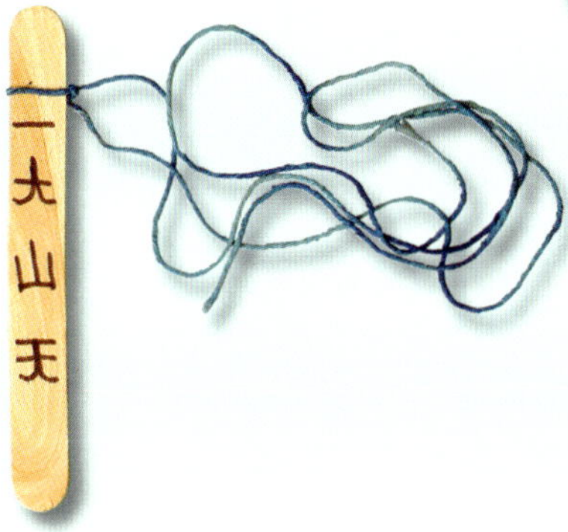

Step Two

Cut two pieces of string about 12 inches (30 cm) long. Tie one of the strings in a knot around the top end of one of the craft sticks. You should end up with even lengths of string on either end of the knot.

Step Three

Place another craft stick next to the first, with thsides of string on either side of the stick. Tie another knot around the second stick. Repeat with the other three craft sticks.

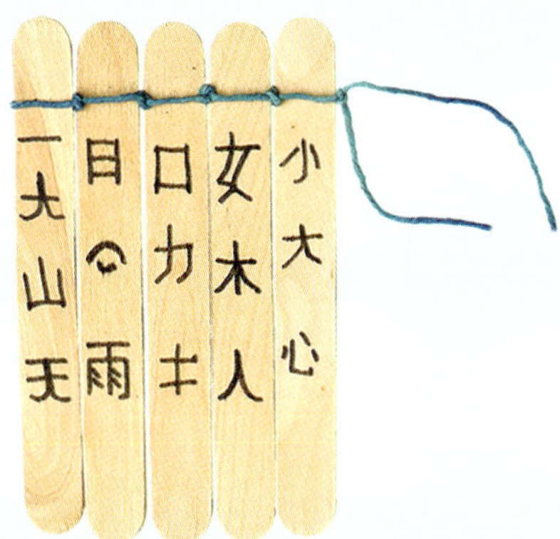

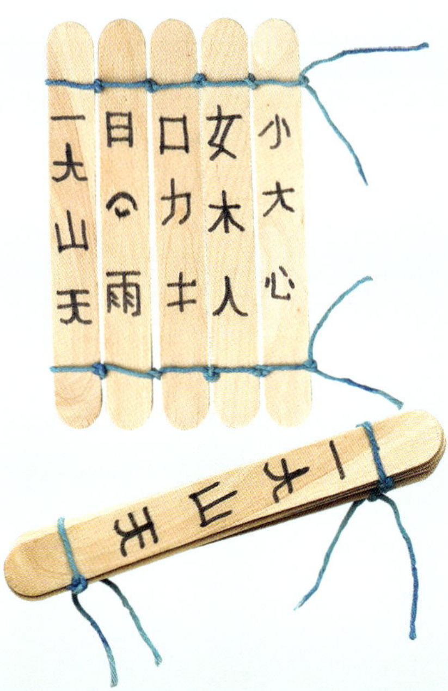

Step Four

Repeat step three with the other piece of string, knotting it around the bottom parts of the craft sticks. Trim the ends of the strings, and fold up your book!

Glossary

ancestors family members who lived long ago

bronze a metal that is a mixture of copper and tin

complex a group of buildings used for a specific purpose

crossbows powerful weapons used to fire arrows

descendants people who are related to others that lived in the past

dynasty a group of rulers from the same family

emperor the ruler of an area

forbidden not allowed

merchants people who sell goods

moat a deep, wide ditch dug around an area or building and filled with water to prevent attacks

mortar a soft building material that is spread between bricks or stones and holds them together when it hardens

mourning feeling very sad for someone who has died

oracle an answer or message delivered by a god through a person or an object

phoenix a legendary bird that was said to burn itself with fire, and then rise from the ashes

scholars people with a lot of knowledge, usually gained from research and study

terra-cotta a reddish-brown clay

unified brought together as one

vessels containers for holding things

Read More

Bell, Samantha S. *Ancient China (Civilizations of the World)*. Lake Elmo, MN: Focus Readers, 2020.

Noll, Elizabeth. *The Great Wall of China (Blastoff! Discovery: The Seven Wonders of the Modern World)*. Minneapolis: Bellwether Media, 2021.

Oachs, Emily Rose. *Ancient China (Blastoff! Discovery: Ancient Civilizations)*. Minneapolis: Bellwether Media, 2020.

Learn More Online

1. Go to **www.factsurfer.com**
2. Enter "**Ancient China**" into the search box.
3. Click on the cover of this book to see a list of websites.

Index

About the Author

Catherine C. Finan is a writer living in northeastern Pennsylvania. She enjoys writing about a wide range of subjects, including ancient history. The Great Wall of China is on her travel bucket list!